A VISIT THROUGH THE *Wetlands*

A Visit Thought the Wetlands - Second Edition
Copyright 2025 - Sherry Roberts
Artwork Copyright 2025 - Sherry Roberts
All Rights Reserved

No part of this book may be reproduced or transmitted in any form or by any means, electronic or mechanical, including photocopying, recording, or by any information storage and retrieval system, without permission in writing from the author.

Clarissa Willis - Publishing Coordinator
Sharon Kizziah-Holmes - Book Design

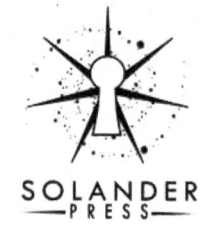

SOLANDER
PRESS

Springdale, Arkansas

ISBN: 978-1-959548-93-5 (Paperback)

A VISIT THROUGH THE *Wetlands*

Sherry Roberts
Author & Photographer

What are Wetlands?

Wetlands are an important part of the ecosystem.
They provide not only land but water for growth.
This makes them a natural ecosystem that is very productive.
Sometimes they have a swampy look to them.
On bright sunny days, you can see the clouds reflect off the water.

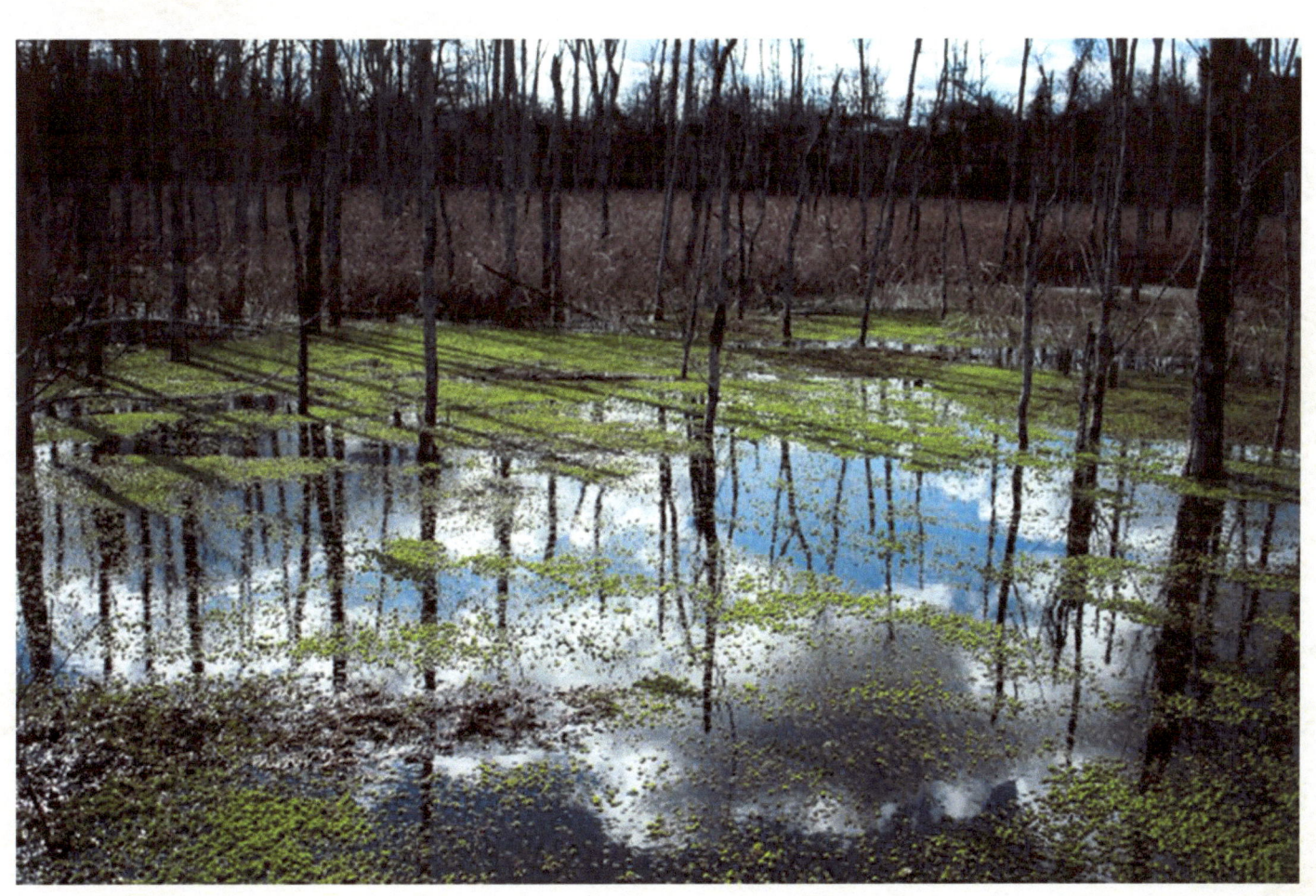

It is fun to walk through local wetlands. Some are very large, some are small. Sometimes they are located within a city park area, while at other times they are part of a swamp area.

You never know what you might find.
Many wetlands have a variety of birds, waterfowl, animals, amphibians, and reptiles.
They also have different vegetation.

Many wetlands provide a beautiful walking path so visitors can view all the inhabitants without disturbing the environment.

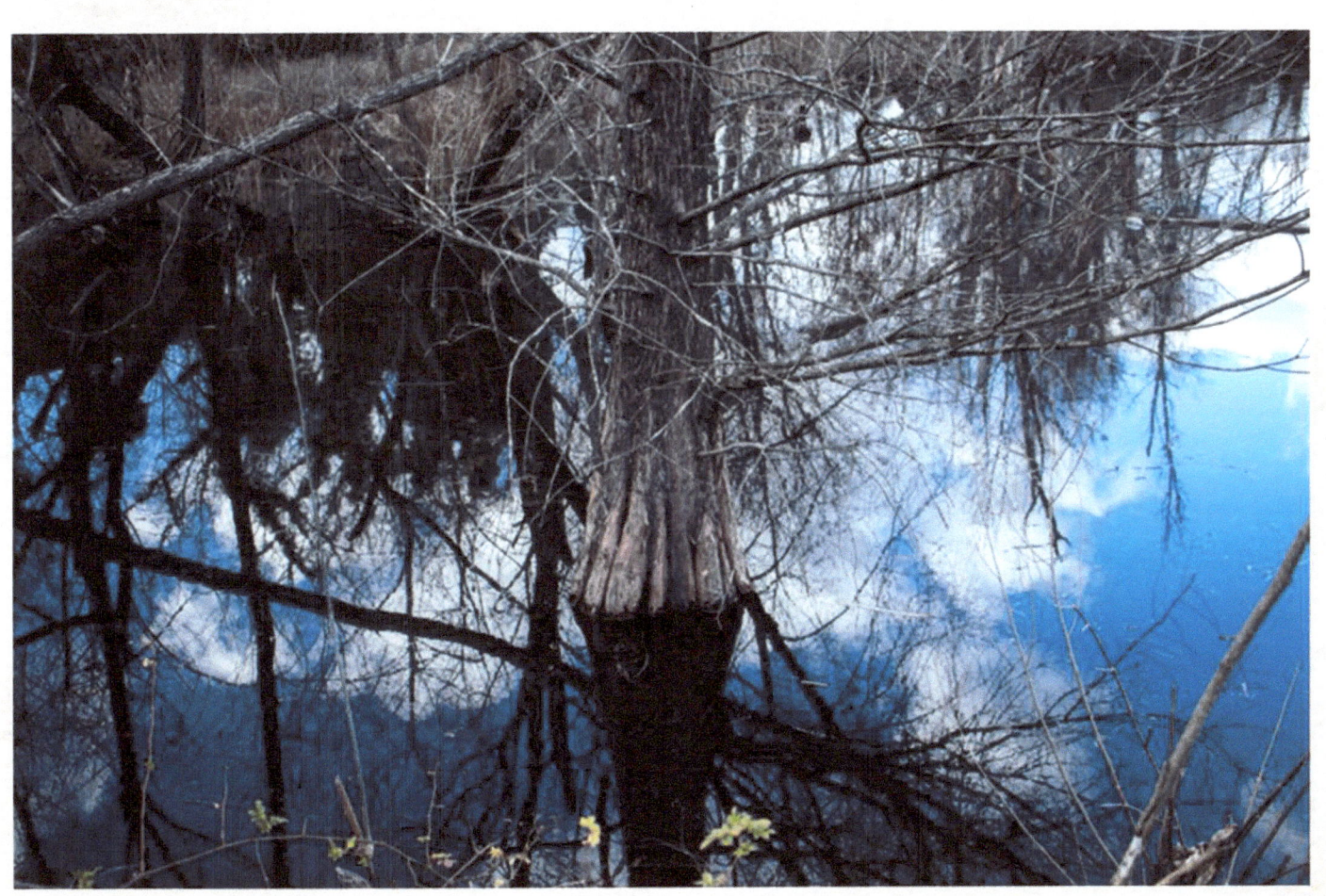

Frogs are not always easy to find in the bog of the wetlands. Their green coloring often blends in with the vegetation within the water.

Here are two pictures of frogs in the vegetation.

Can you find the frog with the flowering vegetation?

One frog was on top of the vegetation and can easily be seen.

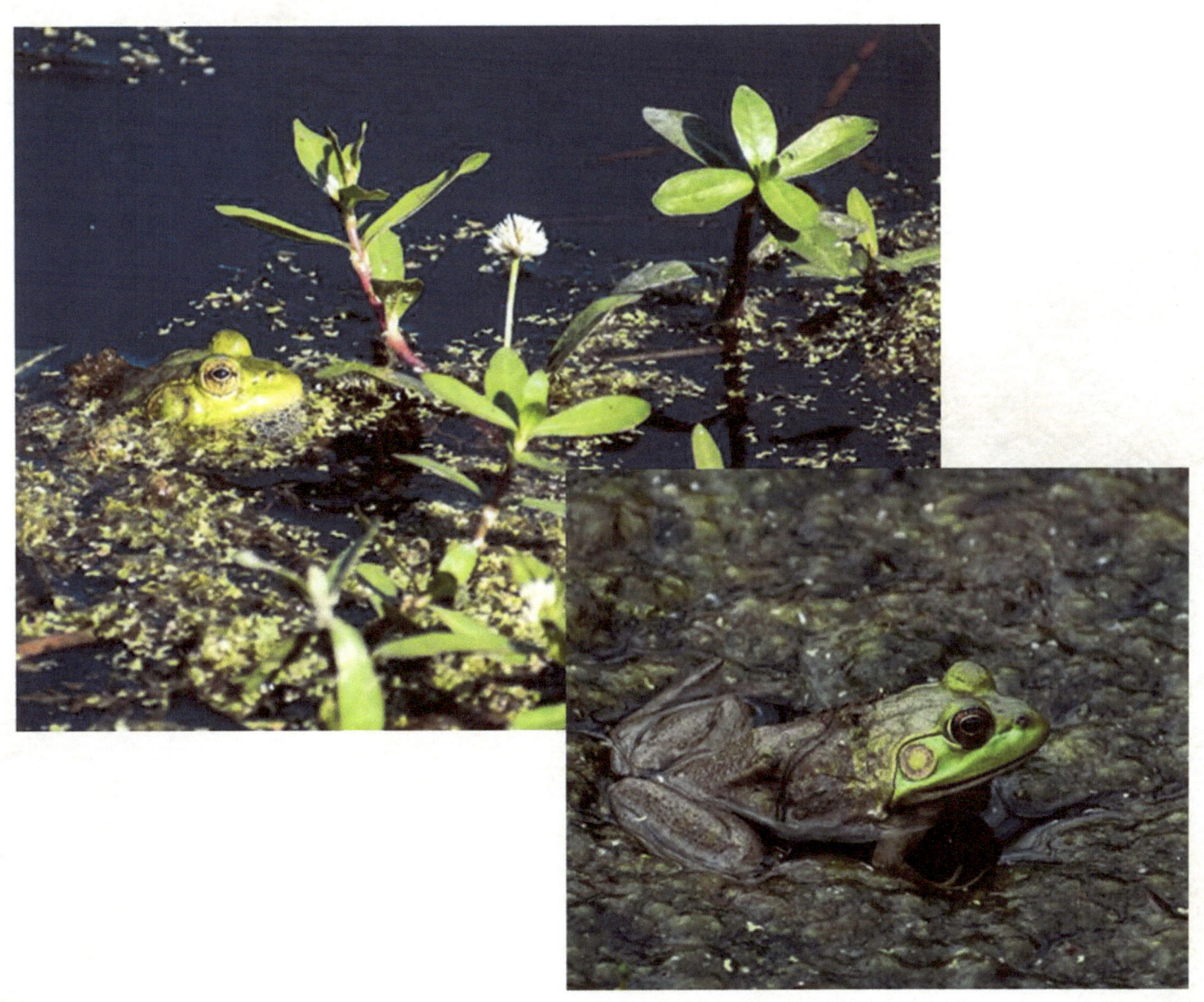

One day you may be walking through and see a turtle or two climbing on a log to bask in the sunshine.

It is not unusual to find a variety of turtles in a wetland area. There might be snapping turtles to alligator turtles.

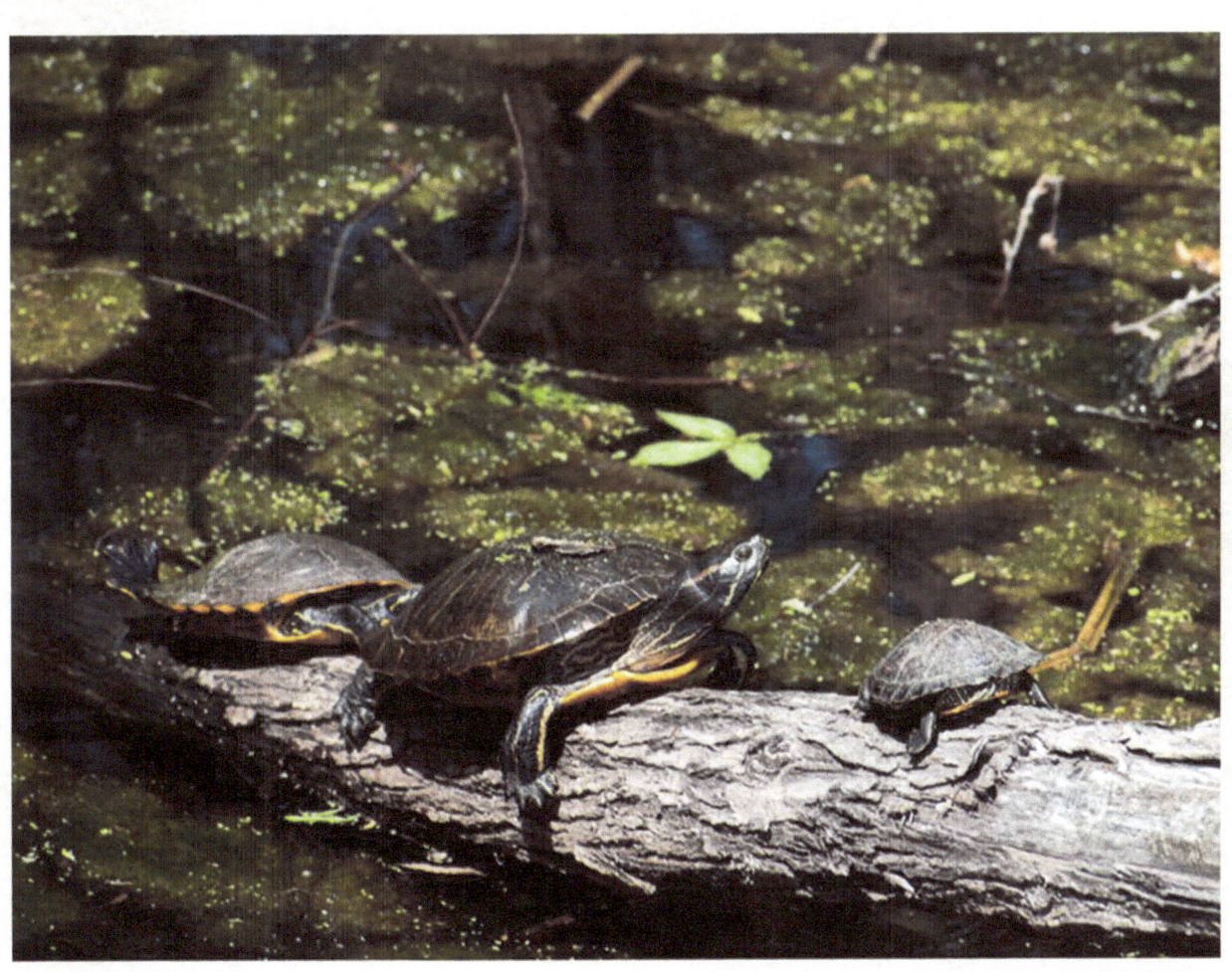

When you are lucky, you might see an otter climb on a log.

Here is an otter who climbed on a log where several turtles were sunning.

"Knock, knock" said the otter to the first turtle.

No answer. All the turtles are hiding in their shells.

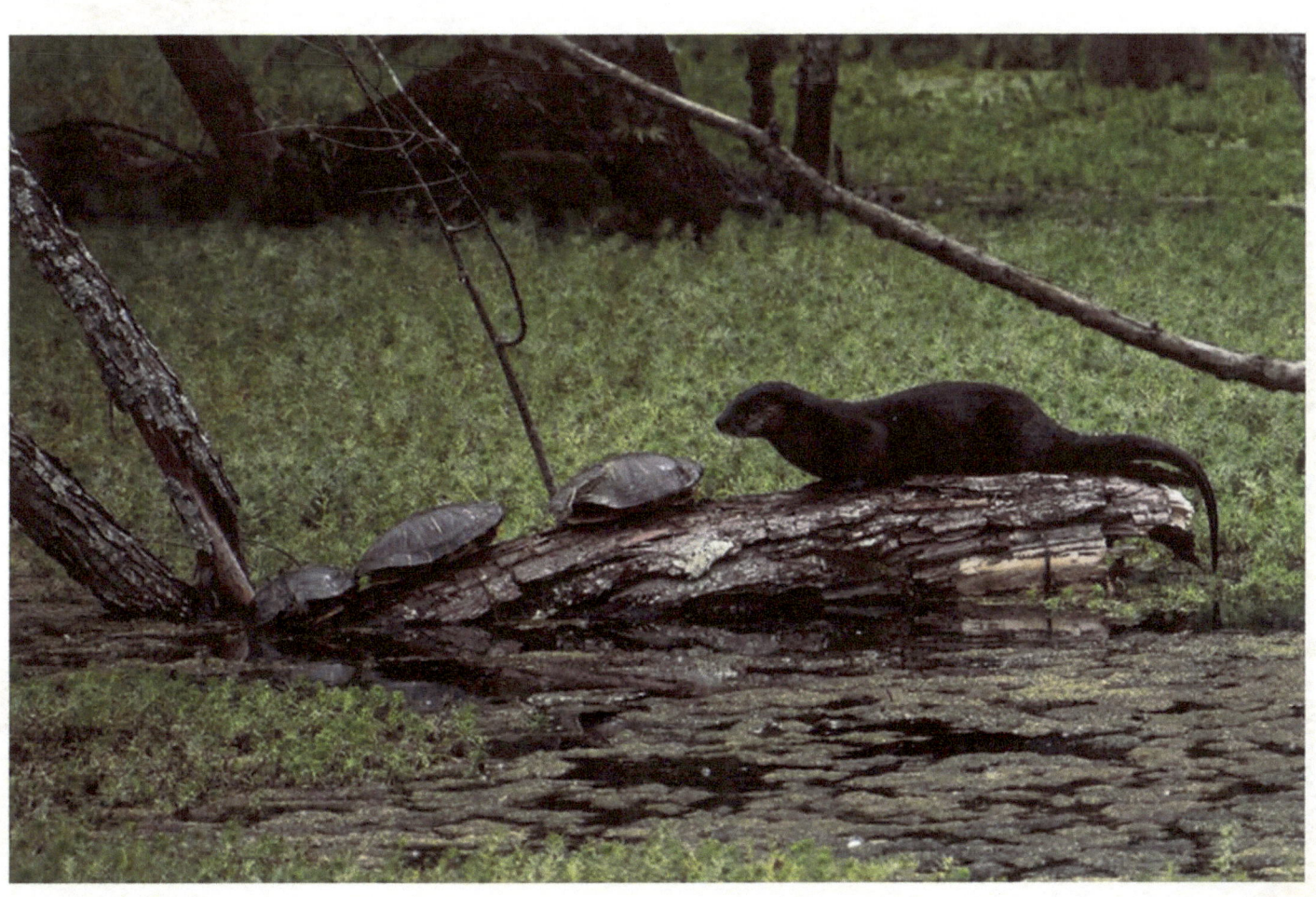

You might see an otter or two swimming and playing in the water.

Otters like to dive in and out of the water, chasing each other.

Here is a family of otters playing in the logs from a beaver dam. As they swim in and out of the water, you can see the shine of their wet coats.

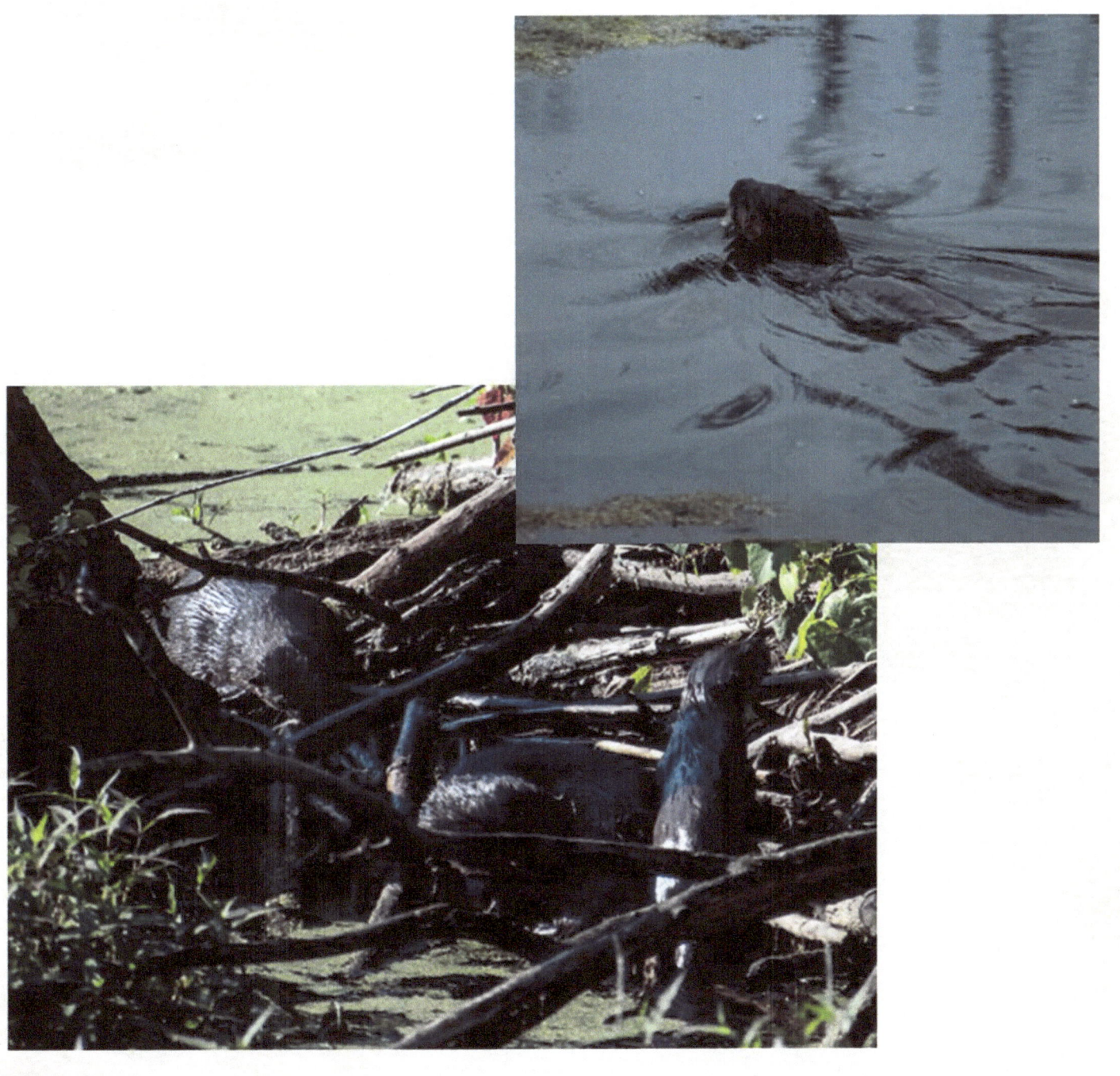

Muskrats can be seen in many wetlands.

They are usually small and can sometimes be mistaken for small or young otters.
Unlike the otter, they do not grow very big and weigh a little over 4 pounds.

Although they do eat small animals, within the wetlands their main source of food is in the vegetation around the wetlands.

Here you see a muskrat having an afternoon snack of vegetations while sitting on a fallen log in the water.

They live in their family of mother, father, and their children.
Their houses are nests built out of the water but feature an underwater entrance to the nest.

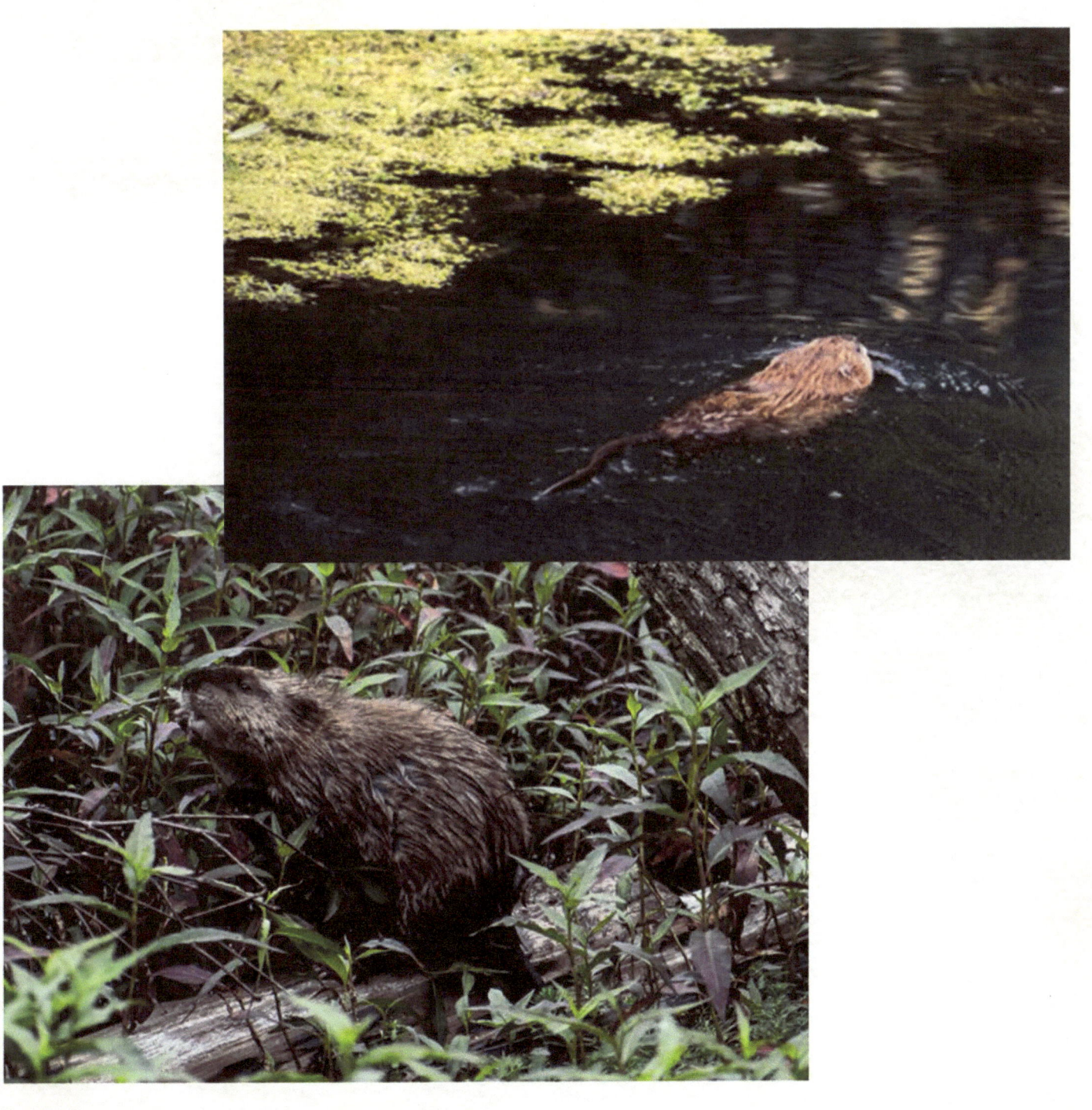

This fat raccoon was wandering through an area of the wetland looking for food.

Raccoons will eat duck eggs, shellfish it might find when digging through the water, turtles and their eggs, or injured birds. They are not really fussy eaters. They are good scavengers whether in the wetlands or even a neighborhood.

Here's another raccoon who found a home in a dead tree. It was a bit hollowed out.
The raccoon hollowed it out more by eating insects that were found within the trunk of the hollow tree.

Climbing up the trunk of the tree, the raccoon looked out to see what the visitors were doing.
It was probably looking to see if anyone had food.

Be sure you do not leave trash or feed any of the animals in the wetlands.

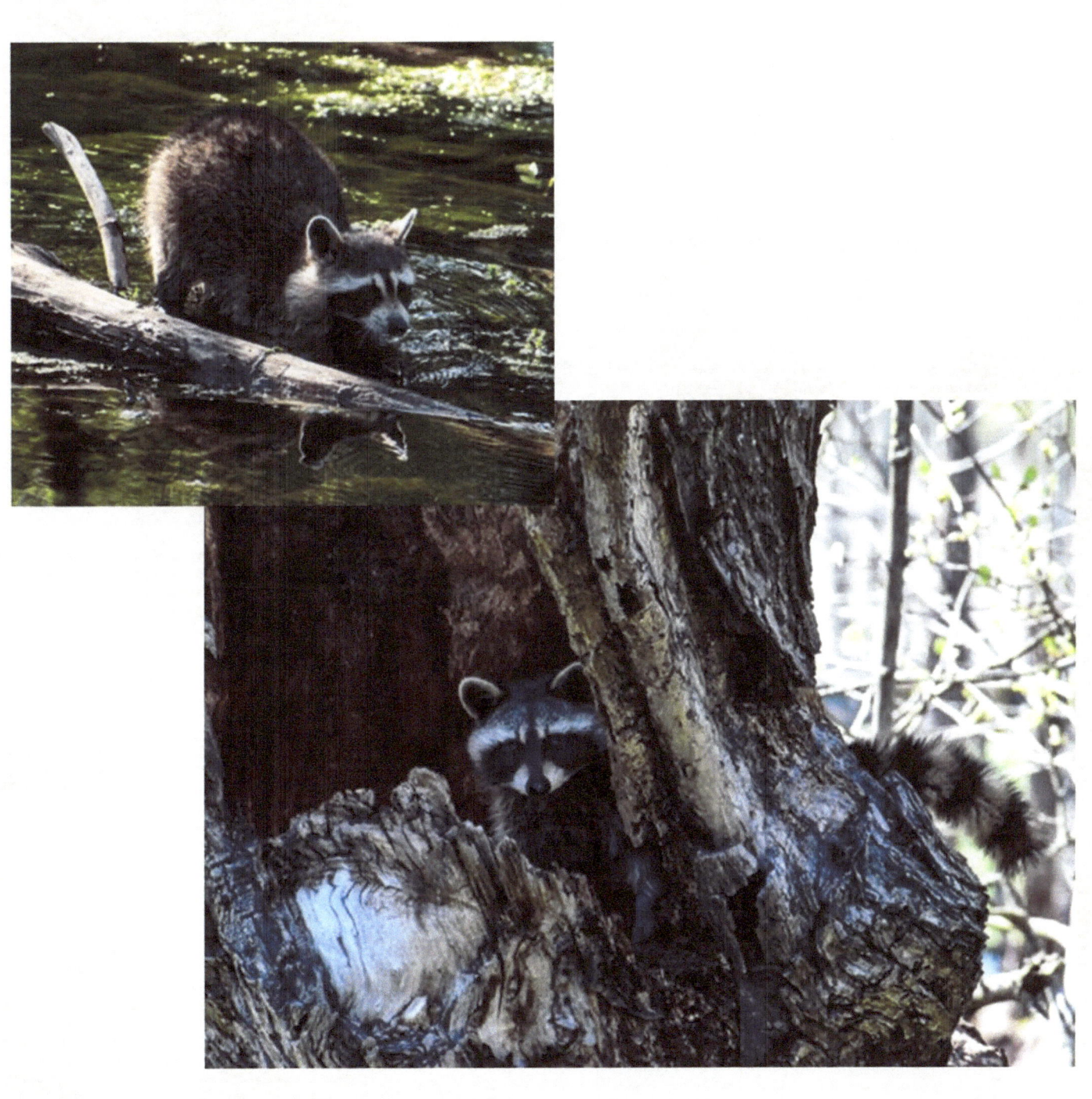

A variety of waterfowl can be found in the wetlands.
What are waterfowl?
This is the group of birds that include all types of ducks, geese, and swans.

Many waterfowl build nests on top of the water around fallen trees or debris from beaver dams.

Here is a little family of Canadian Geese.
Mom and Dad standing guard of the little ones resting.

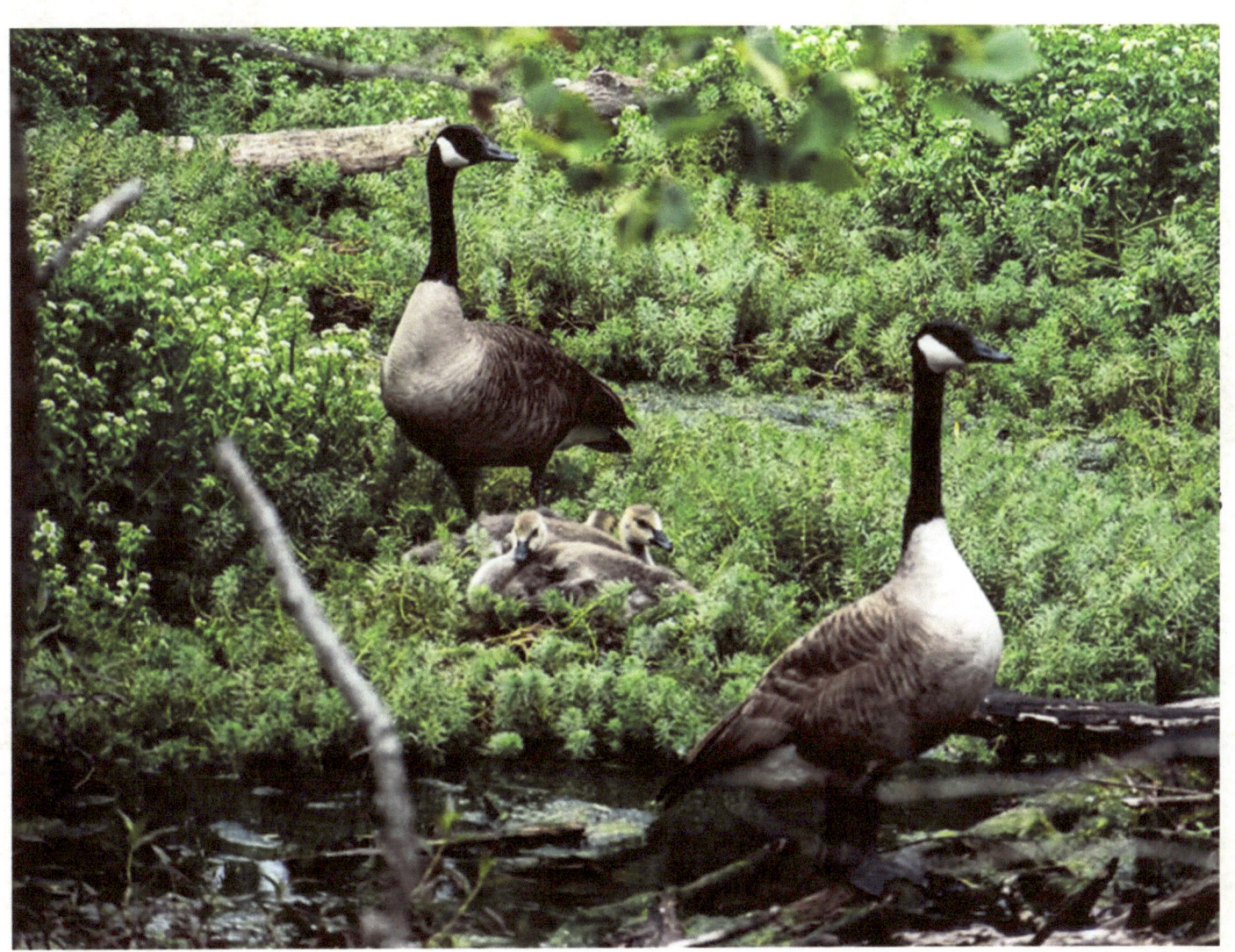

Here are two more waterfowl.

First you have a male mallard duck.
The dark, shiny green head and yellow bill are features of the male mallard duck.
A female mallard duck is less colorful with an orangish-brown bill.
Both male and female have a white-bordered, blue patch on their wing.

The second duck is known as a wood duck.
This is a male. You can tell by his bright colors and patterns in his feathers and his red eyes.
The female has feathers that are more delicate and brownish with sprinkles of white.
The female head plume is not as distinct as the male.

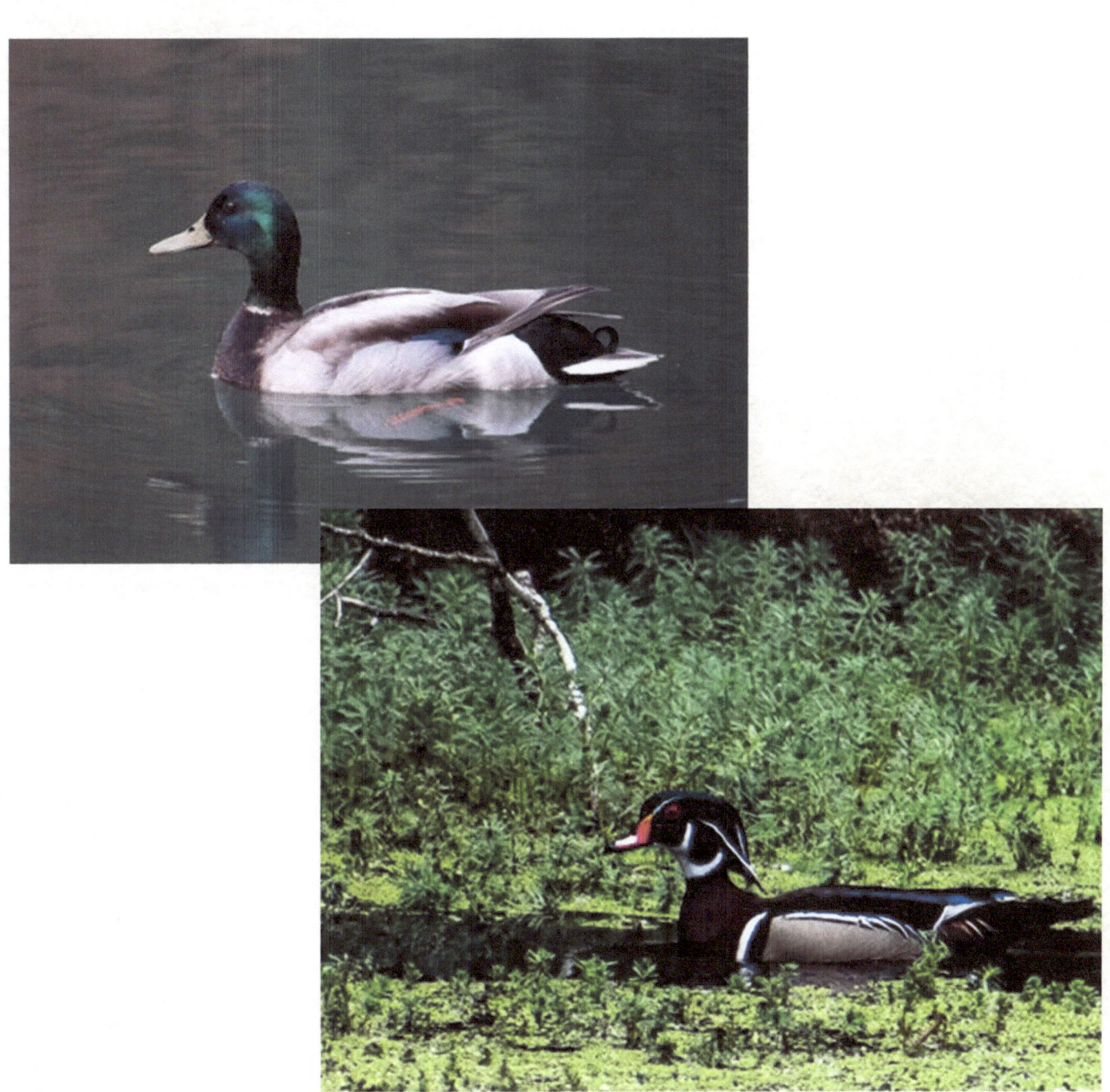

This is a swan goose or white Chinese goose.

They are known for their long necks but also for the bright orange beaks, legs, and feet.
Their iris are maroon in color.

Because of a decline in the population of the swan goose, it is classified as a vulnerable species.

When the swan goose wants to warn off predators, it will give two to three short honks.

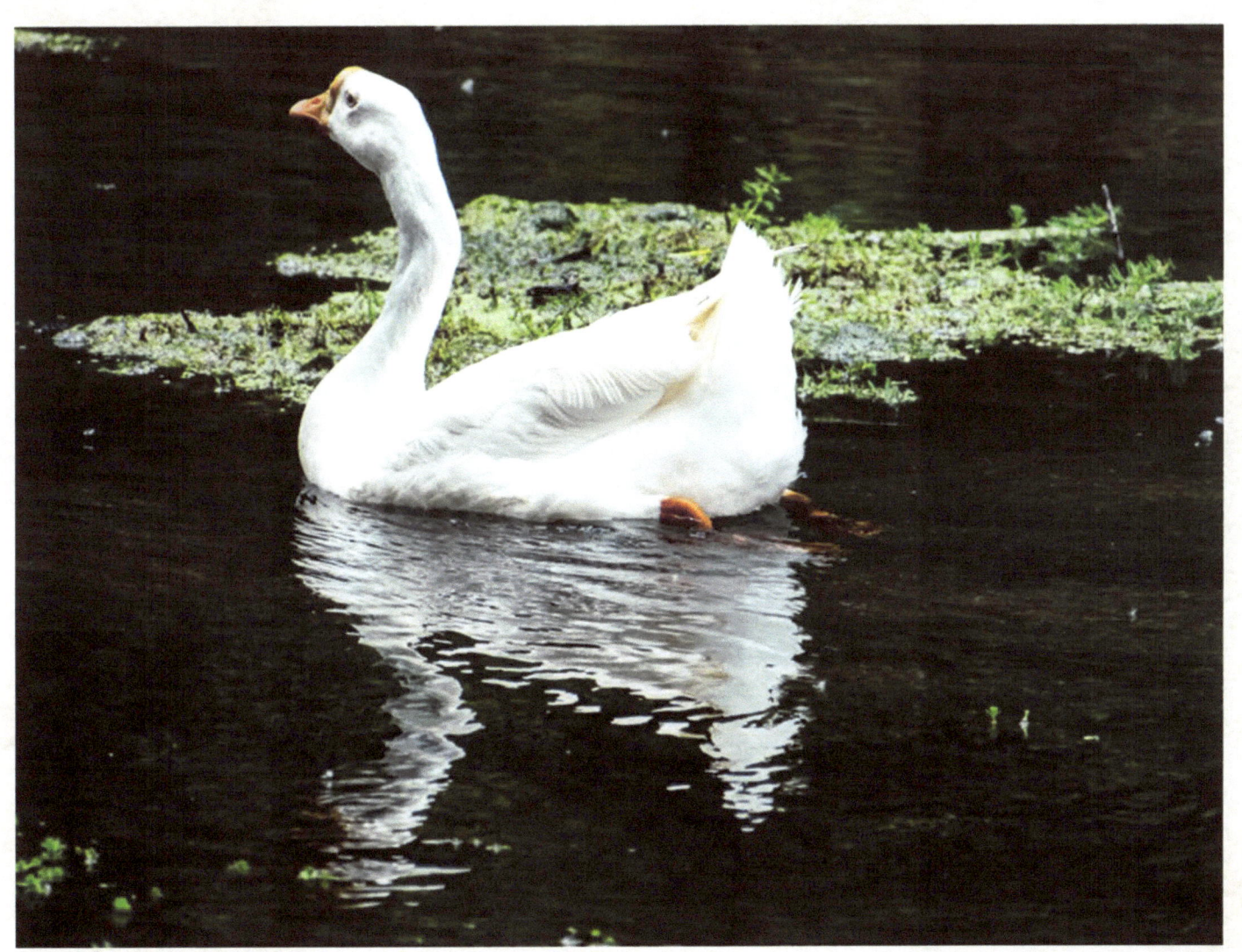

Yellow-Crowned Night Heron are frequent visitors to wetlands areas.

You can tell this waterfowl because of the bright yellow crown on its head.
The adult has bright shades of blue feathers with a dark black and white face.
They build their nests in the trees using broken twigs.

The first picture shows a young, yellow-crowned night heron.

The second picture is of an adult who has just caught a crayfish for dinner.
Yellow-crowned night heron live off crabs and crayfish.
They stalk and lunge into the water to catch their prey.

You might also see Blue Heron and Green Heron in wetlands.

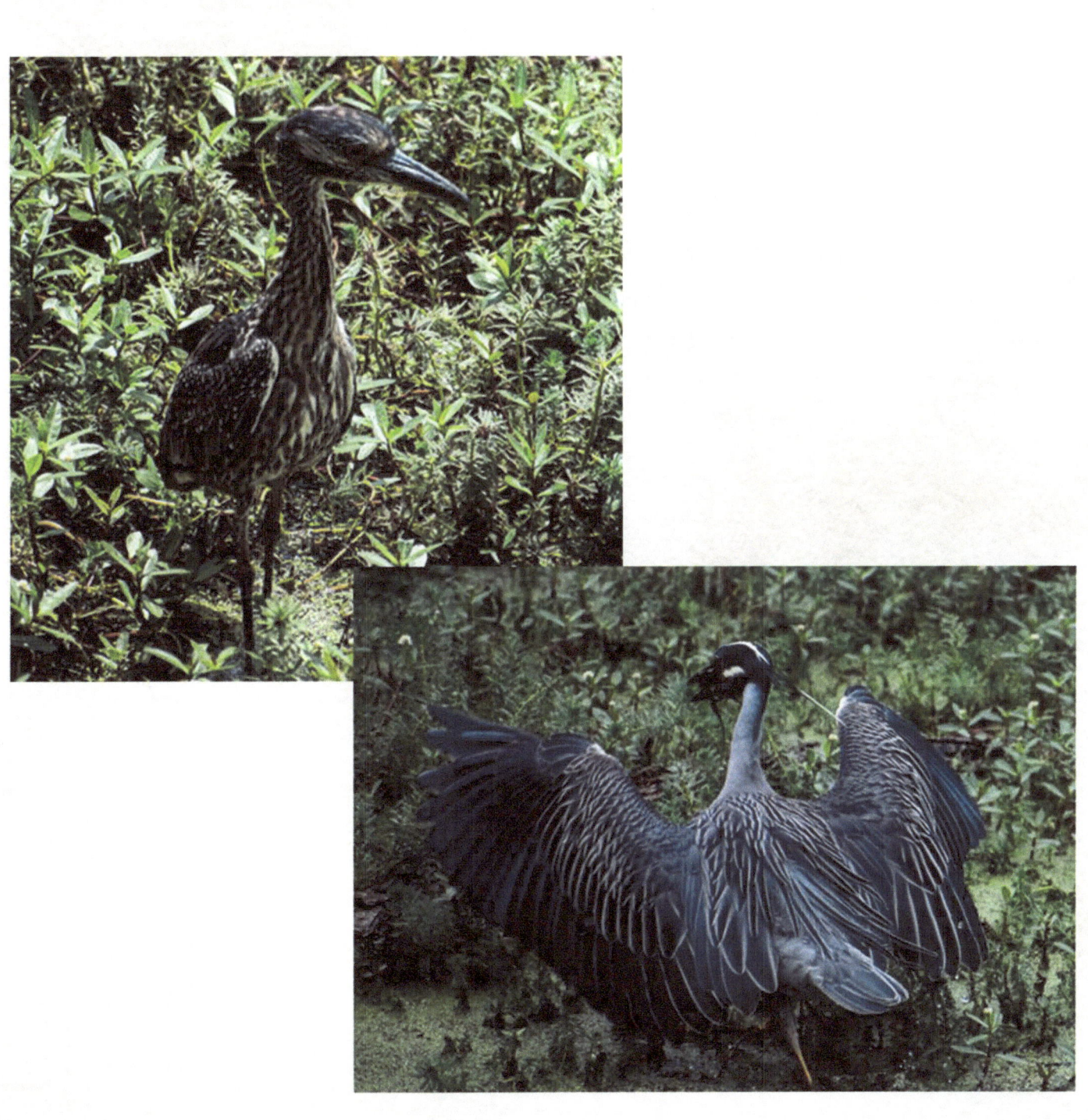

Looking up in the trees, you will see a variety of birds.

Here are just a few found in wetland areas.

A red-winged blackbird known for its shiny black body enhanced by the red and yellow patches on the top of their wings.
It almost looks like they have shoulder pads.

The next bird is an Eastern Kingbird.
They are known by their long blackish tail that ends in white, white breast, and gray-black upper body. One more feature is a small red patch that can be found on their crown.

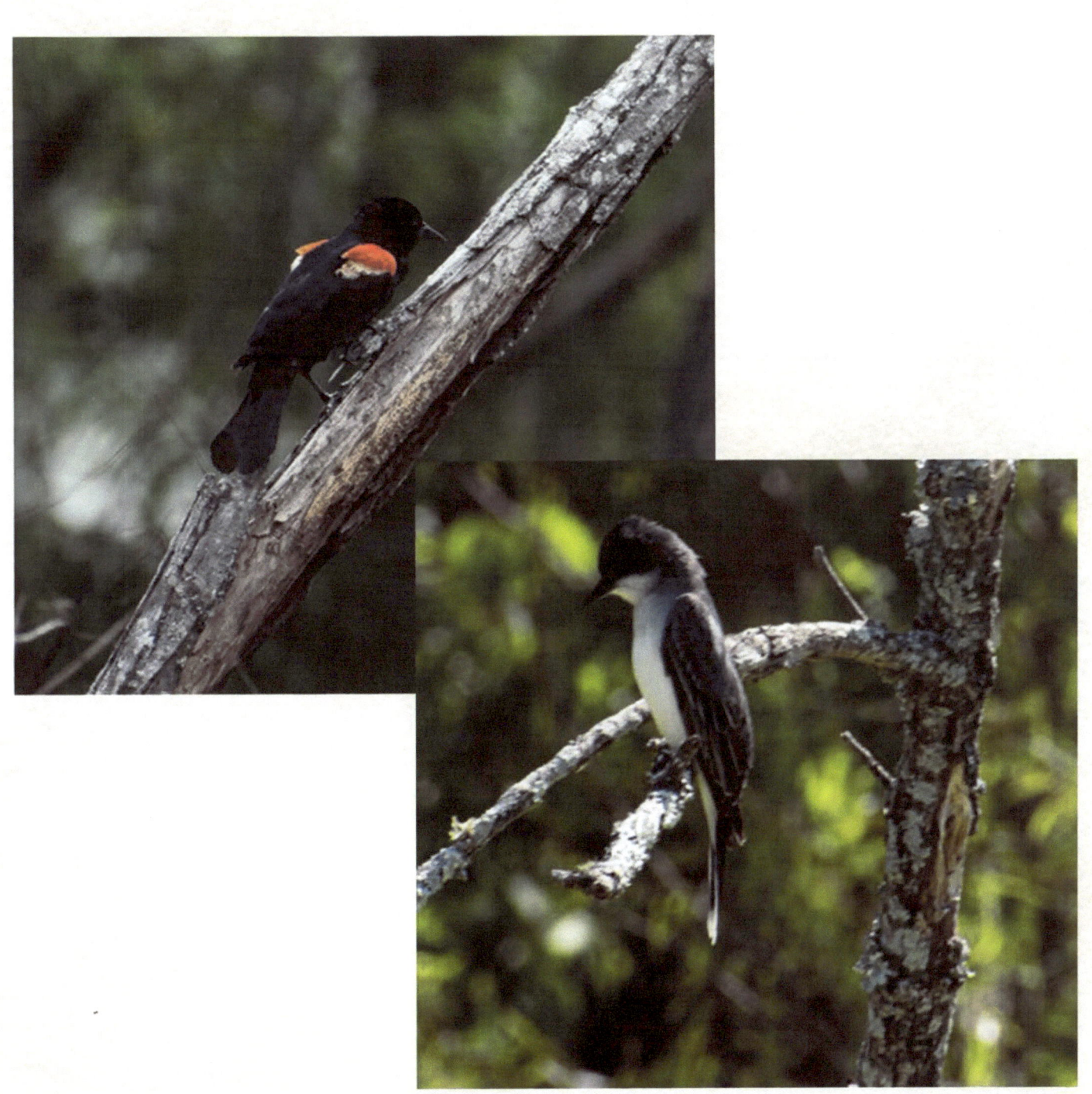

More birds that might be found in the wetlands include downy woodpeckers and rose-breasted finch.

Here you will see a male downy woodpecker.
You can tell it is the male by the red patch on the back of their heads.

The second picture is a rose breasted finch.
This is an adult male.
You can tell by the reddish color of his head, neck, and shoulders.
Sometimes this reddish color will follow through to the breast of the bird.

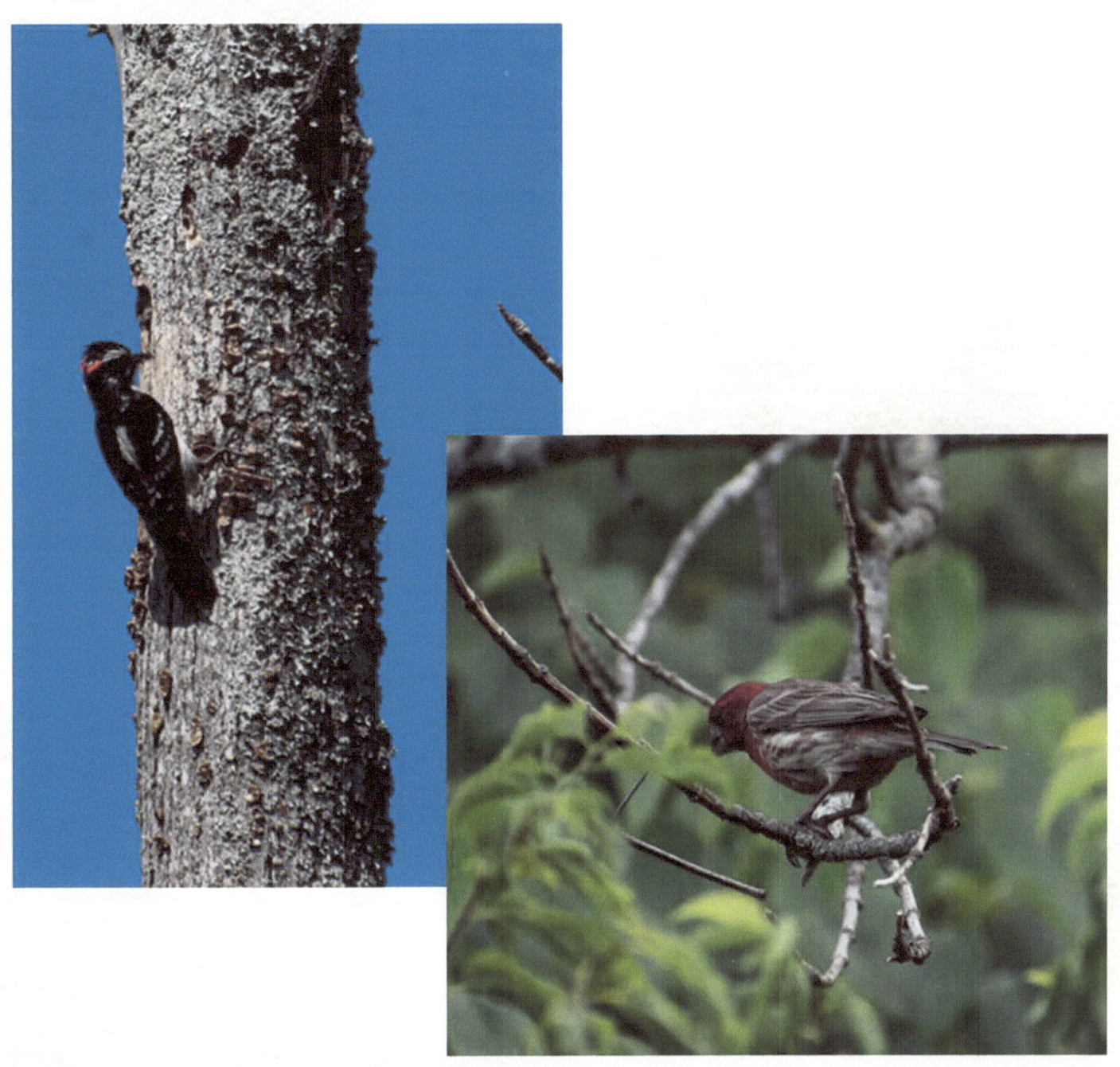

To find out more about wetlands go to

https://www.epa.gov/wetlands/what-wetland

or

http://www.wetlands-initiative.org/what-is-a-wetland

or

https://www.worldwildlife.org/habitats/wetlands

Find wetland areas near you or when visiting an area, find out beforehand if there is a wetlands area close by.

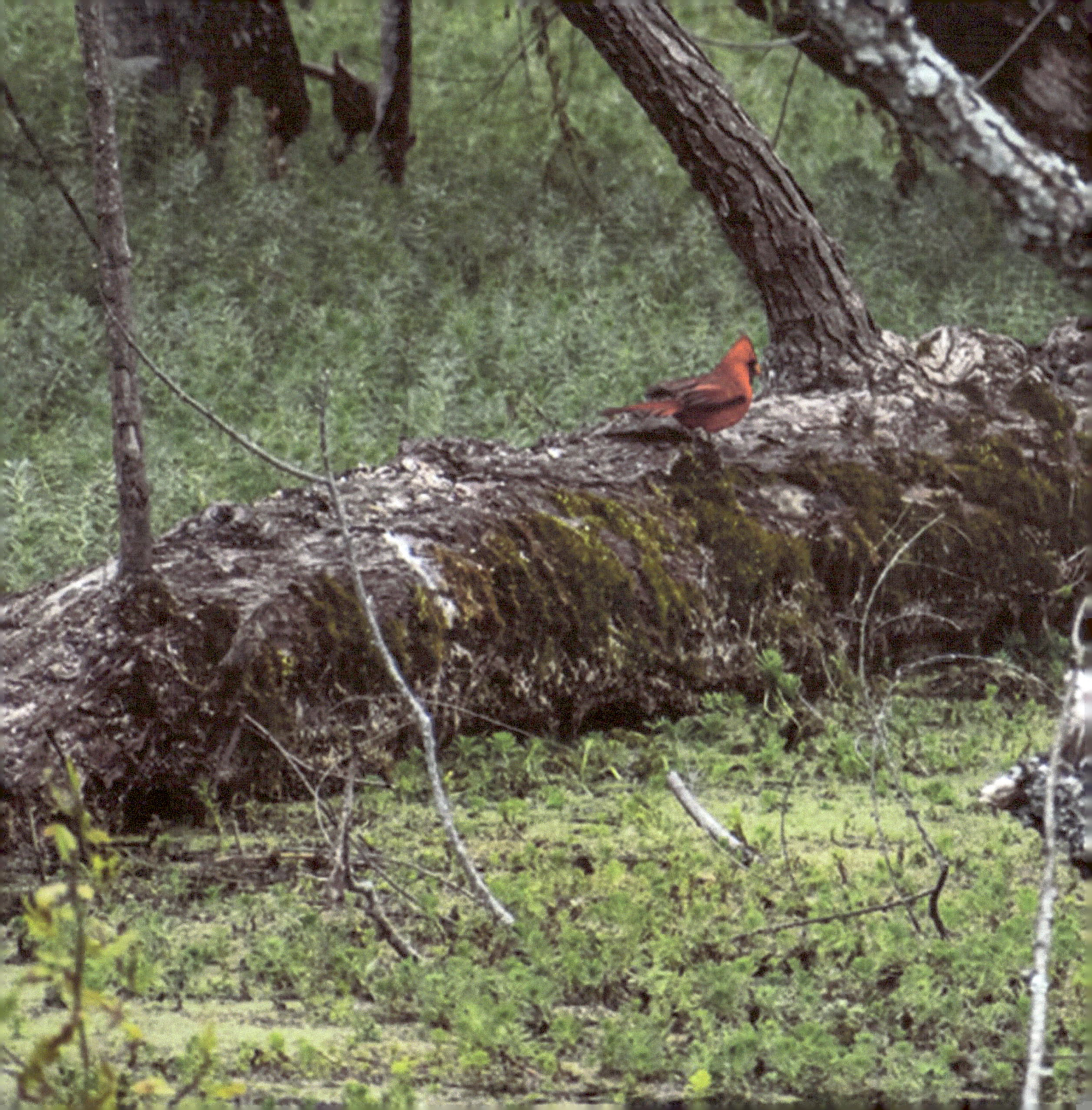

About the Author

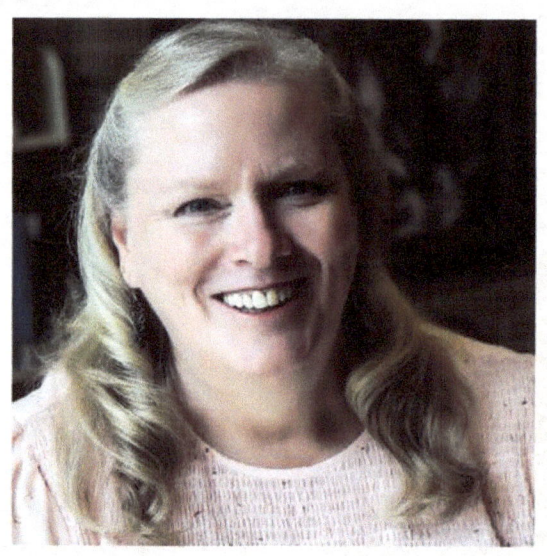

Sherry Roberts is an award-winning children's book author. Creating has always been a life-long adventure for her and making up stories stimulates this creativity. With three nieces and one nephew, she would make-up stories to entertain them. Over the last several years, she began to write picture books. Her creativity also extends to art and photography (as seen in this book) as well. She holds a Ph.D in Curriculum and Instruction from the University of Louisville and has been in the teaching field for over 37 years.

www.ingramcontent.com/pod-product-compliance
Lightning Source LLC
Chambersburg PA
CBHW051818210526
45473CB00005B/1655